How Should I Approach Art?

D1738722

Crucial Questions booklets provide a quick introduction to definitive Christian truths. This expanding collection includes titles such as:

Who Is Jesus?

Can I Trust the Bible?

Does Prayer Change Things?

Can I Know God's Will?

How Should I Live in This World?

What Does It Mean to Be Born Again?

Can I Be Sure I'm Saved?

What Is Faith?

What Can I Do with My Guilt?

What Is the Trinity?

TO BROWSE THE REST OF THE SERIES,
PLEASE VISIT: LIGONIER.ORG/CQ

CQ

How Should I Approach Art?

R.C. SPROUL

 LIGONIER MINISTRIES

How Should I Approach Art?
© 2023 by the R.C. Sproul Trust

Published by Ligonier Ministries
421 Ligonier Court, Sanford, FL 32771
Ligonier.org

Printed in China
Amity Printing Company
0001123

First edition, second printing

ISBN 978-1-64289-443-1 (Paperback)
ISBN 978-1-64289-444-8 (ePub)

Cover design: Ligonier Creative
Interior typeset: Katherine Lloyd, The DESK

Ligonier Ministries edited and adapted Dr. R.C. Sproul's original material to create this volume. We are thankful to Mrs. Vesta Sproul for her invaluable help on this project.

Scripture quotations are from the ESV® Bible (The Holy Bible, English Standard Version®), copyright © 2001 by Crossway, a publishing ministry of Good News Publishers. Used by permission. All rights reserved.

Library of Congress Control Number: 2022930819

Contents

Chapter One

Aesthetics in Recent History

When we look at the role of art in the Christian life and community, we find that there are simple, foundational principles about the nature of beauty. If you were to look up every reference to "beauty" or "the beautiful" in the Bible, you would see that the word "beauty" in one form or another occurs frequently in the pages of sacred Scripture, particularly in the Old Testament. To set a framework for our investigation, let's begin by looking at a psalm written by David, which we find in 1 Chronicles:

Ascribe to the LORD, O families of the peoples,
  ascribe to the LORD glory and strength!
Ascribe to the LORD the glory due his name;
  bring an offering and come before him!
Worship the LORD in the splendor of holiness;
  tremble before him, all the earth;
  yes, the world is established; it shall never be
moved. (1 Chron. 16:28–30)

Two words in this psalm stand out. One is "glory." The idea of the glory of God is pervasive throughout Scripture. It refers to His majesty, His heaviness, His weightiness, His worth, His significance. Closely connected with His glory is the concept of "holiness." The psalm enjoins the people of God to worship God in the "splendor of holiness"; the holiness of God and the glory of God are conjoined here with respect to this idea of splendor or beauty. We are called to come into the presence of God and to worship that which is beautiful about God.

Psalm 27 and Psalm 29 also tell us about this idea of the beauty of God. Psalm 27:4 states:

One thing have I asked of the LORD,
  that will I seek after:

that I may dwell in the house of the LORD
    all the days of my life,
to gaze upon the beauty of the LORD
    and to inquire in his temple.

In Psalm 29, David reiterates what he said in his psalm in 1 Chronicles: we are to worship the Lord in the "splendor of holiness."

I'm afraid that the idea of the beauty of God has been all but eclipsed in our contemporary culture, both in the secular community and in the church. The Scriptures are concerned about three dimensions of the Christian life: the good, the true, and the beautiful. But we have cut off the third from the other two. In fact, sometimes Christians reduce their concern of the things of God purely to the ethical realm, to a discussion of righteousness or goodness. Others are so concerned about purity of doctrine that they're preoccupied with truth at the expense of behavior or of the holy.

I've heard it said, somewhat facetiously, that if you want to find a church that is concerned with the good, you should go to the Baptist community because there morality is emphasized; if you want to be concerned about the true, then you go to the Presbyterians or the Reformed people because they are the ones who spend so much time concerned about doctrine; and if you want to learn about beauty, you have to go to the Episcopal church because there the focus is on the beautiful more than the good or the true. But in fact, the biblical concern is for all three. Scripture tells us that God is the ground or fountain of all goodness. All goodness finds its definition in His being and in His character. What *God* is determines what goodness is. The Scriptures speak about God as the author, the source, and the foundation of all truth. They say that God Himself is true. In the same way and in the same dimension, the Scriptures speak about the beauty of God; all things beautiful find their source and foundation in the character of God. Ultimately, God is the norm of the good, the norm of the true, and the norm of the beautiful.

We are in a time of crisis both in the secular culture and in the church with respect to the beautiful and how it works out in the arts. Christian artists, whether they are musicians, sculptors, painters, architects, or literary people, tell me that they feel cut off from the rest of the Christian community; they tell me that they are treated as pariahs because their vocation is considered somehow worldly and not worthy of Christian devotion. That is a sad commentary on the state of affairs today, particularly when we look at the history of the Christian church. Historically, the church has produced some of the greatest giants in music, art, and literature. In Christian history we find Milton, Handel, Bach, and countless other pioneers of greatness in the arts.

That's not where the scene seems to be today. Part of the reason for this goes back very early in church history to the first iconoclastic controversy, which had to do with the church's use of icons in worship. Great protests arose against the use of icons and created some division between the Eastern church and the Western church. At that time, the question of the use of art in church was raised. The Roman Catholic Church defended its abundant use of art by saying that the art in the church functioned as books for the illiterate. We've heard that "a picture is worth a thousand words," and so in the Middle Ages, one of the ways that the church communicated its doctrines to those who were not literate was through art.

If you were to go to the Louvre Museum in Paris or to the Rijksmuseum in Amsterdam and peruse the history of art, you would see that the works there are dominated by a religious orientation—specifically, a Christian orientation, because art has historically been a central concern of the Christian community. In the Old Testament, the first people who are said to have been filled by the Holy Spirit were the artisans and craftsmen whom God selected to prepare the objects for the tabernacle. These artists were inspired by God the Holy Spirit for their craftsmanship in various media, including furniture, clothing, and metalwork. Aaron's priestly garb was to be made for glory and for beauty. God was concerned not only to use artists in the building of His sanctuary in the Old Testament but also to endow those very artists with the power of His Holy Spirit to make sure that what they were doing met the standards of excellence that He Himself wanted.

At the same time, we also see in the Old Testament strong prohibitions against the misuse of art. One of the Ten Commandments prohibits the making of graven images that become part of a practice of idolatry. So there are forms of art that are forbidden in the Old Testament. Some forms of art received the blessing of God; other forms of art did not. One cannot come to the pages of Scripture with a simplistic conclusion that all art is good or that all art is bad.

But we live after the Old Testament period and also after the Protestant Reformation. Part of the crisis in the Reformation in the sixteenth century involved the use of art in the church. A new iconoclastic movement took hold after the Lutheran Reformation in Germany. After Martin Luther made his famous stand at the Diet of Worms in 1521, he was kidnapped by men on horseback and whisked away into the woods. The kidnapping had been staged by Luther's friends to protect him from the wrath of the emperor. Luther was placed in hiding in the Wartburg Castle.

While Luther was in the Wartburg, word came to him from Wittenberg that one of his chief lieutenants, Andreas Karlstadt, was leading raids against churches. They were smashing stained glass windows and destroying artwork as a revolt against the Roman Catholic Church. Luther left the Wartburg, despite having a price on his head, and returned to Wittenberg to try to stop the rampage against works of art in the churches of Germany. Luther and his colleagues were successful in marginalizing Karlstadt and his followers, so art remained an important part of the worship of the Lutheran community.

Meanwhile, in the Swiss Reformation, John Calvin took a different approach to art in the church. Calvin was in total agreement with Luther about the central significance of the doctrine of justification by faith alone. Calvin also carried a burden to reform the worship of the church. He was convinced that there was a link between the eclipse of the gospel and the practices that he regarded as idolatrous in the medieval Roman Catholic Church. The church had directed its attention away from the Word, away from the gospel, to the sacraments and their trappings found in all the images, statuary, and artwork that was an integral part of the Roman Catholic religion. Calvin sought to reform the church's life and worship by driving out of the church all negative worldly influences of art that would obscure the Word of God.

Calvin acknowledged that art was not inherently wrong. He did not take the position that the Bible outlaws all art in the life of the church, but he said that times were so perilous and that people had become so addicted to the images and statues that were part of the Roman Catholic Church that there had to be a pause in the use of these artworks. People needed to get their attention back to the Word of God and away from these sensuous presentations of art. In fact, when Calvin first came to Geneva, there was no congregational singing whatsoever. When he was later banished from Geneva and went to Strasbourg, he found congregations there singing hymns and psalms, and he saw how much that enhanced their devotion and spirit of worship. When he returned to Geneva, he then allowed music into the worship at Geneva under very strict conditions.

In that Reformed tradition, we saw further hardening against the use of art in the church by the Puritans. One of the things that the Puritans wanted to do was to purify the church from any unbiblical practices that would obscure the purity of the Word of God. In the English Reformation, Puritan pastors lost their jobs, and in some cases were tortured and killed, because they refused to wear the white surplice as part of the priestly garb of the Anglican church. They saw such garments as an unbiblical innovation and contrary to their concern that worship be pleasing and acceptable to God.

The Reformation's response to art involved a reaction against formalism; it was a reaction against externalism and ritualism. In the decay of the medieval church, people were substituting external forms for true religion of the heart and soul. People were just going through the motions. This is the same problem that had emerged in Old Testament Israel, and the prophets had to speak strongly against it.

Jesus was critical of the Pharisees, who were devoted to keeping the forms and doing the externals but who missed the heart and soul of true worship; people put their confidence in the ritual. Jeremiah spoke memorably about such tendencies in his temple speech: "Do not trust in these deceptive words: 'This is the temple of the LORD, the temple of the LORD, the temple of the LORD'" (Jer. 7:4). The people recited the words, but they were lying words that did not profit. The truth of God in the Old Testament was supposed to be mediated and communicated by the external actions involving the tabernacle and the ceremonial rituals that God Himself had devised and introduced to emphasize, enhance, and corroborate the truth of His Word.

In Israel, and then again in the medieval church, the forms, the externals, and the rituals became a substitute for the Word of God. They directed people's attention away from the Scriptures. Israel still had beauty, but without the truth. People therefore became zealous to recover the Word. They said, "We have to not just reform but *deform* the church." The abuse of forms, externals, and rituals led to the ceasing of the use of forms and externals and rituals, which then created a whole new crisis in the life of the church.

Chapter Two

Art for
Whose Sake?

A minister who once visited the church where I preach reacted strenuously against the artwork that is present in our church building. I knew that some people would not like the use of art in Saint Andrew's Chapel. But this man was so upset about it that he wrote to the publisher of some of my books and demanded that it stop publishing my books because of the church's supposedly blasphemous use of art. We may disagree on what kind of art belongs in the church, but it is impossible to remove art completely.

That is because every form is an art form, and every art form communicates something.

We ended chapter 1 by examining the reaction in church history against formalism, externalism, and ritualism. The same critiques that were leveled against these problems in the sixteenth-century Reformation were also raised by the reformers of the Old Testament—the prophets of Israel. It's important for us to understand that the prophets of Israel were not iconoclasts. They did not try to get rid of the forms, externals, or rituals because they understood that these had been ordained by God. The problem wasn't with rituals or forms or externals; the problem was with what people were doing with rituals.

Any ritual, as rich as it may be in its origin, may lose its meaning by mindless repetition. We can recite the Lord's Prayer by rote and completely miss the content; we can turn it into an empty ritual. Yet the cure to externalism and ritualism, according to the prophets, was not to throw out the forms, externals, and rituals but to reform them and continue to associate the Word to the sign. Throughout redemptive history, God has always added sacrament to Word, some kind of visual or auditory aid to enhance the significance of the Word. The Bible comes to us not simply through verbal communication but through that which is perceived through our senses. All the way back to the Noahic covenant, God promised never to destroy the world again by flood. To corroborate His Word, He set His bow in the sky as His outward, external, formal sign, guaranteeing the content of His word. But as soon as you lose the verbal content, then the signs and the externals degenerate into godless formalism.

There's another reason that the prophets didn't do away with the externals and all the art from worship: it simply can't be done. There is no possible escape from art or from externals or from liturgy in corporate worship because corporate worship has to take place somewhere, and forms are involved wherever you worship. You may choose to have a church that is as plain in its ornamentation as possible, but it's still using art forms.

For example, think of a lectern used by a preacher. You might think that it's there just to hold up his Bible and his notes, that it is purely functional and utilitarian, that it has no aesthetic dimension. But if you look at a typical lectern, you'll see little details that aren't necessary for simply holding a Bible. It is probably finished in some way rather than being made of rough, unfinished wood. There might be trim on the column or the bottom. It's probably stained an attractive color rather than painted yellow with polka dots. A lectern like this might be simple and neutral, but it still contains an art aspect and an aesthetic dimension.

All forms are art forms, and every art form communicates something. If I walk into a church that is completely plain and unadorned, there's a message to me from that plain and unadorned church. We've seen in our day an attempt to de-churchify church, to remove all the accoutrements of churchiness from church buildings, because we think that this modern generation doesn't want to be invited into old, outmoded, traditional houses of worship that look like churches. So the architecture changes dramatically. A traditional church might have a chancel with a large central pulpit, while a modern church might have a stage with a simple lectern that can be moved to make way for other things. A traditional church might meet in a sanctuary, while a modern church might meet in a worship center. The decisions around these elements reflect a certain way of thinking about worship, and thus the elements communicate a certain message.

Medieval cathedrals were built to communicate a particular message. As you walk into such a cathedral, you can see that the entryway is darker than the nave and that clerestory windows let light into the sanctuary. The idea is to communicate that you're walking from the darkness of this world into the light of the presence of God. Even when people can't articulate this, in many cases they feel it nevertheless.

By contrast, you have a different feeling when you walk into a town hall or a civic meeting center, and many modern churches are now being built after that model. The idea is to make people comfortable, to have a place where they can come without fear, enjoy fellowship, and not be inhibited by any threat of a transcendent, holy God. So all the symbols of transcendence and holiness are removed to make room for creature comfort. But there is the danger that a sense of the transcendence of God has been eclipsed in the life of the church.

Most people say that it doesn't matter. Isn't God looking for people to worship Him in spirit and truth (John 4:24)? It doesn't matter if you worship Him in a tent, or if you worship Him outside, or if you worship Him in a storefront, or if you worship Him in a medieval cathedral. God does not require that He be worshiped in a Gothic cathedral. But when you pitch that tent, that tent is going to communicate something. It is important to remember that no matter what you do, you are choosing an art form, and that art form is communicating something.

The question is not whether there will be art forms in church—you can't have church without them—or whether you're going to have ritual. Even in a Quaker meeting, where there is no order of worship and people simply speak as they are moved, there is still some kind of order and regular sequence that goes on. Every church has a liturgy. Every church has externals. Every church has forms. So the question is not whether we're going to have church with forms or without forms, with liturgy or not. The issue is whether the forms are good forms, are beautiful forms, are true forms. Do they enhance the truth and the goodness and the beautiful, or are they bad forms? It's not whether we're going to have art or not have art; it's whether the art that we have is good art or bad art, whether it's beautiful or whether it's ugly, whether it's symphony or cacophony, whether it's order and cosmos or disorder and chaos. That's why I think it's important for the Christian community to examine the matter of beauty. Just as we study what is good and true, we also need to be studying what is beautiful.

God is not only the author and inspirer of art, but He Himself is an artist. In a very simple way, we observe that every single day. God is an artist who doesn't need paint or brushes or a canvas, but by the power of His word He can create worlds of beauty, fill empty voids with real things, and triumph over the unformed abyss by speaking the word of creation.

Sometimes the sunsets in Florida are so spectacular, they're breathtaking. Even after you've been looking at sunsets all your life, you can see a sunset that is so incredibly beautiful that it stops you in your tracks. You can look down into the Grand Canyon and be in awe. You fly over the Rockies in the winter and see the snow-capped peaks. In all these things and more, you can see the hand of the Creator in the design work.

Consider the sea. I've been mesmerized watching the sun and the waves on the sea, watching the hues and shades change by the second. God is an artist. He's a clothier. He's a cobbler. The deer lives his whole life with one coat, and the coat serves him whether it's hot or cold, whether it's snowy or rainy. He doesn't have to run down the street to buy a new overcoat; his coat lasts him as long as he lives. He has one pair of shoes, and the shoes are magnificent.

We can pick any other example from nature and see how God clothes the lilies, how He clothes the sparrow, how He gives beauty and glory to all kinds of diverse things in the world that He makes. Not only is He the source of art, but He Himself is the greatest artist in the history of creation. In this book, we're going to see whether we can find transcendent norms within God Himself that give us clues about what is beautiful and what isn't.

Chapter Three

Is Beauty in the Eye of the Beholder?

As we continue with our study of the Christian and the arts, we turn our attention to the age-old debate over the nature of aesthetics: Is beauty discerned purely subjectively, or are there external, objective standards or criteria by which something may be judged to be beautiful? We are living in a period in Western history that favors subjectivism. You've no doubt heard the cliché "Beauty is in the eye of the beholder." More and more, people argue that there are no ultimate standards for beauty. This should not surprise us, because we have seen a denial of objectivity across the board. We've seen a denial of objective truth and of objective goodness. Philosophies center on the core belief that truth itself is subjective and that there are no absolutes—except the absolute that there are absolutely no absolutes. Society insists that we have truths but no truth, beauties but no beauty, purposes but no purpose. This creates quite a bit of confusion when we come to this question of the nature of beauty.

In every aesthetic experience a person has, there is a subjective response, and it is certainly clear that each one of us has his or her preferences with respect to art. Some of us like one type of music while others like a different kind, or one style of painting, and so on. No one would want to argue that there's no involvement of the responding subject to the realm of art. But we're still asking the question, "Is there anything beyond our subjective feelings, personal preferences, and individual responses to that which we consider beautiful that can be seen as some kind of objective basis for beauty?" The battle is not only between the subjective and the objective but also between the normative and the relative.

We know that language shifts in the culture. Today, the word *value* substitutes for the classic word *ethic*. When people say that we have lost a sense of values, they mean that we're engaged in some kind of ethical crisis, because the norms that determine right conduct and proper behavior in the past have been set aside and replaced by the principle of relativism. Yet the irony is that, historically, value has been sharply distinguished from ethics and has been almost universally acknowledged to be subjective. The subjective theory of value says that the way that you value your car will not be exactly the same way that your neighbor values your car or even the way that your neighbor values his own car. We all have different sets of values in terms of the worth or importance that we assign to certain elements of our experience.

One could argue from the Christian perspective that there is such a thing as a normative value. The worth that God attaches to certain things would be the supreme standard of value, and the Christian should try to get his or her personal values in line with God's values. But the normative says "ought." When we talk about norms, we're talking about standards that impose on us some kind of ethical imperative, some kind of obligation. So when it comes to the arts, we ask, "Is there a kind of art that so corresponds to norms found in the character of God that we ought to appreciate it, even though we might not appreciate it now?" In the course of study known as art appreciation, the goal is to instill a higher sense of appreciation for deeper forms of art because such forms of art are considered to be more in harmony with classical norms and standards for beauty.

If indeed God is the foundation of beauty, and if there are norms for beauty that are grounded in the character of God, then that imposes on us an obligation to seek to understand the elements of those norms and to embrace those norms for ourselves rather than depending on our own private preferences to determine what is beautiful and what isn't.

Part of this issue of norms for aesthetics is the debate over the difference between chaos and cosmos. The astronomer Carl Sagan became famous with his television program *Cosmos* and his best-selling book by the same name. In the beginning of the book, Sagan comes at questions of reality from the perspective of one who believes that scientific knowledge is indeed possible and that what makes scientific knowledge possible is the fact that the universe in which we live is *cosmos*. That is, it is a place with an inherently built-in systemic order, one that is knowable by the careful observer. Sagan follows the principle of epistemology that undergirded the Enlightenment, which sought, by use of the scientific method, to discover "the logic of the facts." In other words, the Enlightenment thinkers were saying that we're bombarded every day by a myriad of details, little data bits of our experience, and we must ask: "How do they relate to one another? How do they fit together?" Through experimentation and research, one can try to find patterns, forms, and hints to the logic by which these things hang together.

We are now living in the most antilogical period in Western history. People reject logic even though they can't live without it. Sagan understood that without order, without cosmos, there are no patterns, and that if there are no patterns, no structures, no standards or norms, then what you have is chaos. The problem for the scientist is that chaos is unintelligible. Even the movement in science called "chaos theory" is an attempt to study apparent chaos by looking at it more closely in order to reveal its underlying structure.

Imagine that you're on an ocean liner. You stand at the edge of the rail, you look into the water, and you see the water swirling around as the boat moves through the ocean. You focus on one set of bubbles, one little piece of foam, and you try to follow it. You try to watch how it behaves and predict where it's going to go next. So many factors are interacting here—the currents and the winds and so on—that to the naked eye, it's almost impossible to predict where it's going to go next. Yet chaos scientists say that there are principles and laws at work here and that, in fact, there is a harmony of what's taking place even in this seemingly chaotic response of gases and fluids and so on in the universe. Even in chaos theory we find the assumption that science is cosmos; there is order.

That presupposes a formal structure to things. At the entrance of Plato's Academy was a sign that read, "Let none but geometers enter here." Wasn't Plato a philosopher, not a mathematician? Did that mean that you had to have a Ph.D. in geometry to get into Plato's Academy? No, by "geometers," he meant people who were committed to the study of form in its mathematical relationship and proportionality. Plato had been deeply influenced by the Pythagoreans, who had developed a philosophy of numbers in which everything in reality was explained mathematically. Great breakthroughs of science over the ages have been pioneered by forward-thinking mathematicians who found a simpler math or a more complete math and followed where it led. That was the case with Einstein, Newton, Copernicus, and a host of other scientists who were pioneers because of their conviction of a rational, harmonious inner structure of reality that could be communicated in terms of the logic of mathematics. In a sense, mathematics is symbolic; it's a form of symbolic logic.

Plato, following the Pythagoreans, was concerned to discover the harmony of the world, particularly the heavens, where the ancient astronomers believed that the so-called harmony of the spheres resided. They believed that the stars, in their order, spelled out a certain majestic harmony that could be known, and they followed the course of the planets. Plotting the motion of planets and stars and the phases of the moon was crucial to the ancient person, particularly in an agrarian society where planting and harvesting were determined not by calendars but by the movements of the stars in the sky.

Aristotle, the great student of Plato, was the supreme scientist of antiquity. His star student was Alexander the Great. Alexander shared Aristotle's passion for unity, and so at Aristotle's behest, when Alexander went on his world-conquering crusades with his army, he took with him battalions of scientists to collect samples of flora and fauna along the way. It's been said that the most expensive scientific expedition in history (until the American space program) was Alexander the Great's scientific attempt to capture samples for Aristotle's scientific research. Aristotle was an encyclopedic genius whose knowledge was not focused on only one field; he wrote in a learned way in philosophy, biology, physics, drama, ethics, and other subjects. In examining reality, Aristotle sought to discover the transcendent norms of beauty, and he isolated certain factors that he said are common to the beautiful.

Aristotle's work was later echoed from a Christian perspective in the Middle Ages by Thomas Aquinas. Thomas emphasized basically the same principles of beauty that Aristotle had introduced earlier, and that was picked up and employed later in eighteenth-century America by Jonathan Edwards. In his aesthetic theory, Edwards incorporated most of these same principles as normative standards.

Aristotle pointed to the basic principles of proportion, harmony, simplicity, and complexity as the basis of beauty, so that beauty is based not on arbitrary feelings or on chaos but on the interaction of these basic principles. In the 1960s, a composer named John Cage tried to compose music in a way that was completely arbitrary, with no mathematical significance. He was trying to make a statement that music or art is completely random, completely by chance. There is no form; there is no order. The work he produced is strange. Yet the irony of Cage, as Francis Schaeffer once pointed out, was that his avocation was that he was a gourmet mushroom collector, and when he would go into the forest to collect his mushrooms, he never did it randomly or arbitrarily. He followed certain criteria or standards to find good mushrooms and avoid dangerous ones. In reality, he couldn't live with the principle that he was trying to communicate with his art—that life is completely chaotic.

But these basic principles of proportion, harmony, simplicity, and complexity can be found in the art of painting, sculpture, dance, music, literature, and all the other various art forms that we know. First, when we think about proportion, we think about the difference between primitive art and advanced art, the difference between a symphony and noise. I don't have to be a Matisse to make a beautiful stick figure. But if I want to turn my stick figure into a portrait of a human, then I have to worry about the relationship of the hands to the ankles to the nose to the ears—and all of a sudden, portraiture becomes much more complicated.

There is real skill in someone who is able to produce works of art that are not chaotic, that have proportion.

Second, proportion is related to harmony. Harmony occurs when the pieces that are used in a given work of art fit together in an integrated way. They're not garish. The difference between music and noise can be discerned on the basis of harmony.

Third is simplicity. Something doesn't have to be complex to be beautiful. A certain beauty is found in a Gregorian chant that has no harmony, or in plainsong, or in anything else that is simple. But they are not simplistic. Even in the simple, relationship is still involved.

Finally, we have complexity. It's one thing for me to take a tin whistle and play a little tune. It's quite another thing to add to it bassoons, oboes, violins, and violas to create an entire symphony, with many different parts and instruments playing at the same time and yet maintaining a harmonious relationship. That doesn't happen randomly. These are the things that we're going to explore in the coming chapters.

Chapter Four

The Influence
of Music

We hear many sounds every day. We hear birds, or we hear the wind as it whistles across the landscape. The sounds we hear have a powerful ability to affect the heart and the soul—that is, to affect our moods and our behavioral patterns. This necessitates caution, especially when it comes to music. Even Plato was concerned about the popular music of his time because of the tremendous impact it had on the behavior of the young people of Athens.

When I look back to my own youth, I think about how much of our youth culture was conditioned, if not determined, by the popular music of our day. We were all, as it were, slaves to the radio shows that played nothing but popular music. We knew all the disc jockeys. One of the great inventions of my adolescence was the portable radio. We wouldn't go anywhere without carrying those large-handled portable radios with us.

Sound plays an important role in our daily lives, and every sound we hear has a pitch. Music is made when tones of various pitches are combined, either in a sequence—do, re, mi, fa, so, la, ti, do—or at the same time in harmony.

The music we listened to when I was a teenager is considered funny and ridiculous these days because we didn't have what's popular today; in our day, we mostly had ballads. Love songs were dominant in popular music and informed how boys and girls in their adolescence interacted with each other. Not only that, but these songs created an atmosphere and a rhythm by which people were able to dance. Not only did we listen to this music, but we learned a specific form of dancing to go along with that music. Dancing when music is playing appears to be a very natural response; I've watched infants begin to move and simulate a dance pattern as they listen to different forms of music.

People use music intentionally to create moods. Again, back in the fifties, mood music was important. We had music to iron your clothes by, or to dine by, or to ride the elevator by. We had music coming into the dentist's office to provide a comforting sound to our ears that would perhaps drown out the terrifying sound of the dentist's drill. But this is not new; from all history, people have understood that music has a powerful influence on human behavior. Think back to the Old Testament and the explosive temper and madness that King Saul suffered (1 Sam. 16). To calm his spirit, he would bring David in to play music because his music was soothing. You've heard the saying that music soothes the savage beast. Music can be used to calm the spirit, to excite the sensual desires of people, and to cause people to jump for joy.

I've observed music used in greenhouses to promote the growth of plants. Some say that even plants are in tune to certain forms of music. If you want to know how music is used to create moods, pay attention to the soundtrack of the next movie you see. When was the last time you saw a movie that didn't have a soundtrack? The movie—the visual dimension—is one thing that's going on, but it is enhanced by the soundtrack that carries the motion picture along. When you hear eerie, mysterious music, you know that it's time to watch out because something suspenseful and scary is about to happen. I still can't hear the "William Tell Overture" without thinking of the Lone Ranger, because that was the theme song for the radio production of *The Lone Ranger*.

When we talk about music, we are talking about something different from noise. A jackhammer may emit a specific tone when it's tearing up the sidewalk, but we don't usually associate it with music. Music is more sophisticated. And here is where we run into the principles of aesthetics that we mentioned in the previous chapter: proportion, harmony, simplicity, and complexity. The basic elements that make up music as we know it involve the elements of melody, harmony, rhythm, timbre, texture, form, and some others. Timbre has to do with how the sound is influenced by the instrument or the mode in which it's expressed. For example, if you hear the tone of B-flat played on the piano, it sounds one way. If you hear a B-flat played by a violin, it's the same note, the same tone, but it sounds different because the timbre of a violin is different from the timbre of a piano. Instruments themselves add to the variations we hear in music.

The first tune that I learned on the piano was called "Middle C." It started off with the index finger of the right hand touching middle C, and I had to sing along with it, "I am playing middle C." Then I shifted to the left hand: "I can play it well, you see." The whole song was composed of one note repeated all the way through. It was a song because there was a sequence of tones, and so it did have a melody (even though it was the same tone). But it wasn't a very interesting melody. It was a simplistic melody.

There are virtually an infinite number of ways that you can relate individual tones to each other. There are twelve tones in an octave, but it's not as if we have only twelve ways of producing them. We can take those twelve tones and relate them in millions of different ways. That's why there are always new songs; new melodies are created every day.

In addition to melodies, there is harmony, when more than one tone is played at the same time. There are chords and tritones and even chord fragments. There is a mathematical relationship between the tones that are used to make up chords. When your child discovers the piano in your living room and starts banging on it, hitting several notes at the same time, you notice immediately that what you're hearing is not music. That is because all the principles of proportionality and intervals that make up proper harmony have been violated, and now that sound is reduced to an irritating noise. It's not yet really what we call music. Harmony has to do with a mathematical relationship between the tones that are used simultaneously.

After hearing about the principles of melody, harmony, and rhythm, someone asked me about jazz, because jazz doesn't have any of those elements. This person assumed that jazz has no proportionality, no harmony, no melody, and no complexity. I responded that jazz does have all those things. The harmonies are just different. It is true that jazz is spontaneous. In fact, the definition of jazz is improvisation. But there are different ways of improvising music. You can change the rhythm from the way it's written but still use an ordered, rational, mathematical rhythm, and you can move off the harmony that was written for a song and create new harmonies that have elements of dissonance, and so on, but the structure of modern jazz still follows strict mathematical relationships.

That doesn't mean that every jazz player understands and can articulate those mathematical intervals. The ones who are classically trained and become jazz musicians understand. But those who play jazz by ear still hear the relationships of those sounds, which are mathematically in harmony. They just sound different from the usual way. Western music is primarily built on chords of thirds. A simple C major chord—C, E, and G—is built first of all on a major third, and then on top of that is a minor third. That's the way all the major chords are built. If you want to make it a minor chord, you start with a minor third, and on top of that is a major third, and so on, and you have your basic chord. Even when music might sound strange to your ear, the harmony still has a mathematical proportion. Even in progressive forms of music, the principles of order and harmony are there.

Chapter Five

Music:
The Handmaiden
of Theology

We have seen that we can apply the classical standards of beauty (proportion, harmony, simplicity, complexity) to music—even, as we saw in the previous chapter, to jazz. Though jazz employs improvisation, it does not resort to chaos. In jazz, we encounter an improvisation of rhythm; a song may be written with a particular rhythm in mind, but the jazz musician will change the original rhythm. Yet it still operates in a rational manner.

We also find in modern jazz what's called *melodic improvisation*. When you listen to jazz musicians, you will hear riffs, which depart from the traditional melody line. The saxophone or the clarinet or the piano will go away from the regular melody and play some funky melody, yet that melody still corresponds mathematically to the basic structure of the song that is being played; it's not completely free from structure or form.

In fact, many jazz players have first been accomplished classicists in their approach to music. Not only do they know the simple major and minor scales that we associate with music, but they also pay attention to other kinds of scales, such as what are known as modal scales. For example, in the key of C, the progression is C, D, E, F, G, A, B, C—do, re, mi, fa, so, la, ti, do. But other kinds of scales can be related to the same key signature, called different modes of the original scale, and they can get very complicated. There's the Phrygian mode and the Mixolydian mode, among others. Many jazz players have mastered the different modes of the scales, and they play them against the basic key signature. So what sounds like pure spontaneity is done with the mathematical relationship intact.

The same thing occurs with harmony. When we talk about harmony, we talk about the relationship of multiple tones. Usually, a major chord has three tones, but you can build on those three and have more tones in the chord that make it fuller, richer, and at times more dissonant. When we talk about these major chords, we measure them mathematically in terms of intervals; an interval is the length between the notes in a chord. We number this space between notes with the Arabic numeric system, so that you have the number one note, and the number three note, and the number five note on the scale. And so all major chords are built on that same relationship. If I were to take the D chord, I would start with number one, being D, and the third step interval from that would be F-sharp, and then A. Again, it's one, three, five. Whatever key you're in follows that same numerical sequence. Now, you can add tones to these basic triads. For instance, you can add a major sixth, which in this case would be an A, or you can add a minor seventh, which is a B-flat, or a major seventh, which is a B, and even up to ninths, elevenths, and thirteenths. That is what you get in jazz. You get enriched chords that add to the basic structure of the music, and as strange as it may sound to us, it still follows a definitive mathematical pattern.

In popular American music, the simplest way to play a tune is by restricting the chords to three: the one chord, the four chord, and the five chord. Any teenager who has learned how to strum a guitar learned this principle because you can play almost every song there is with just three chords: the tonic chord, which is the one chord; the subdominant chord, which is the four chord; and the dominant seventh, which is the five chord. You go in this progression: you plunk on the C, then you plunk on the F, then you plunk on the G7. The five chord drives the music back to the foundation, back to the C chord. So when you hear that dominant seventh chord, it signals the ear to anticipate that the next chord you will hear will be the tonic chord. Again, it doesn't always happen that way, but it's common.

Jazz (and classical) music gets far more complicated than this simple arrangement. One of the problems with pop music is its lack of complexity, the sameness of sounds. A person can lead worship music with a guitar and know only three chords and just keep strumming those three chords. Much of what passes for popular music and what occurs in church music is simplistic.

In church music today, we've seen a revolution: the introduction of so-called praise music as distinguished from classical hymnody. When we look at the elements of praise music in our churches today, we see some things that are very good and some things that are problematic. Personally, I like a wide variety of music. I like gospel music, and I like country-and-western music. I like pop, jazz, classical choral music, bluegrass, and opera. Just about every kind of music there is, I like it, so I can't be accused of being fixated on one style of music. I loved popular music when I was a kid, and I still like popular music, particularly from that era. But I notice that when I listen to popular music, even my heroes and favorites, I can listen to it for only so long until it begins to bore me.

By contrast, the more I listen to Bach or Mozart, the richer the music becomes to me. I begin to experience more nuances of sound as my ear starts to unlock some of the complexity that's missing from the simple music that becomes popular for a moment before fading into obscurity. The reason that classical music is called classical is that it has endured the test of time. That music has a richness, a depth of content that continues to awaken the stirring of the soul as these elements of beauty become more and more recognizable in our experience.

There is a place for the very simple in worship, however. We wouldn't go on the mission field, introduce Christianity to a different culture, and right away say "We want you to worship with Handel and Mendelssohn and Bach" if they've had no prior experience in classical music.

There is a simplicity that goes with infancy, and yet as we grow up, we're expected to grow deeper as well as older. The Bible talks to us about leaving the elemental things aside and growing up into maturity, not being satisfied with milk, as we were when we were infants, but developing a taste for meat. That same distinction can be made with respect to music. That doesn't mean that somebody has to be a sophisticated master of classical repertoire to worship God in a way that is pleasing to Him, but as we grow in our understanding of God, that growth should be enhanced by our understanding of the music we use to accompany our worship. I know that people, particularly young Christians and new Christians, are deeply moved by singing praise songs. In fact, they sometimes almost swoon in their enjoyment of it. I can enjoy a praise song sometimes, but there has to be more than that as we grow in our understanding of the things of God. And that is a controversy in the church today.

Jonathan Edwards is often thought of as a preacher who talked about hell, wrath, and judgment. But somebody once did a vocabulary analysis of all of Edwards' works and discovered that the two nouns he used the most were "sweetness" and "excellence." When he talked about sweetness and excellence, he was talking about the character of God and of Christ. In *Religious Affections*, Edwards writes that what happens in conversion is not simply intellectual but a radical change in the heart, a change in the disposition of the soul. Before, a person was indifferent toward the things of God or Christ, but through the work of the Holy Spirit in conversion, that person now sees the loveliness of Christ, the sweetness of Christ. In a real sense, the conversion of the soul is an aesthetic experience, when the soul is awakened to the beauty of God and the soul falls in love with that God. Music can be a way of fanning that affection for God in worship.

I realize that all music that's ever been used in a church was, at one time, contemporary. The issue today is not over new music versus old music; it's over good music versus mediocre music. If we are to grow in maturity, we should try to use the greatest, richest music we can find to elevate the soul to a worship of the beauty of God. Martin Luther said that the handmaiden of theology is music and that music has a powerful impact on the worship experience of the people of God. That is why it is dangerous to take simplistic music from the world and bring it into the church without adapting that music to its purpose in worship. This is a serious mistake that the church is making in our day.

Part of today's controversy has to do with the appearance of an invasion of worldliness into the house of God. We have seen a move in church music to reach out to a more and more secularized world as a means of evangelism, to speak to people in their own language, to give them music that they can relate to. Some people cite a statement that was supposedly made by Luther (but it wasn't): "Why should the devil have all the good music?" They argue that Luther got his music from the bars of Germany, which couldn't be further from the truth. Luther was a true musician, and he did not borrow music from the alehouses of Germany.

We design worship to make it more attractive to the unbeliever, calling it seeker-sensitive. This is partly rooted in the evangelistic tradition of American mass evangelism, in which, at evangelistic rallies and meetings, music other than traditional hymnody was used. Special music helped support the evangelists, and it was music that the public could relate to without having been steeped in Christian heritage. That kind of music was seen as somewhat effective in helping the ministry of evangelism. But then we must ask: "What is the purpose of worship on Sunday morning? Is it to do evangelism, or is it the assembling together of the saints for worship?" Whether we see Sunday morning as an evangelistic outreach mission or as a worship service, the way that we look at our worship services will determine how we structure them. I am convinced that the purpose of Sunday-morning worship is for the praise of God and the edification of His people. Afterward, those people are supposed to then go out into the highways and byways and do the work of evangelism, but the primary function of Sunday-morning worship is to offer the sacrifice of praise to God.

Seeker-sensitive worship assumes that people who are unbelievers are seeking after God, when the Bible tells us without any ambiguity that the unbeliever is not seeking after God but is seeking the benefits that only God can give him while at the same time fleeing the immediate presence of God. There is a particular theology that drives seeker-sensitive worship, but people today are making no connection between their understanding of God and their understanding of how He is to be approached in worship.

Chapter Six

Literature and the Christian

Our view of Christianity and the arts not only affects how we worship God on Sunday, but it also affects our understanding of the relationship between art and culture. My book *The Consequences of Ideas* was developed from a course on the history of philosophy that I taught. In this book, I explain that philosophical systems created by intellectuals result in alternative worldviews that have an impact on culture. People behave the way they think, and they behave according to how they perceive the world and how they understand life. So the history of philosophy is the history of the articulation of competing systems of thought or worldviews, which are usually created in intellectual ivory towers, and we wonder whether they have any relevance whatsoever to culture.

For the most part, in the history of Western civilization, the technical ideas of the philosophers have escaped from the ivory tower and into the public square through intermediaries called *artists*. If you study the history of painting, music, architecture, or any of the other arts, you soon see that movements in the world of art tend to follow shifts in the world of philosophy—that is, the history of art mirrors the history of philosophy. When rationalism reigned supreme in the seventeenth century, it was manifested by the artists' neoclassicism in their music and writing. We see this throughout Western history. It's the artists who are the real change agents that introduce ideas into the culture. We don't want to think for a minute that the popular music, literature, or paintings that we see have no philosophical content. On the contrary, these styles and forms of art are delivery mechanisms to awaken people to new ways of thinking and acting. This is why we have to be careful about what we borrow from the secular world and bring into the Christian life, not just in terms of music but also in terms of painting, architecture, and literature.

Literacy rates in the Western world are higher than ever, but people are actually less adept at reading today than the generations that came before. Images have become paramount, along with short, pithy texts. Books and long-form analysis are passé. Political campaigns are run not on the basis of carefully reasoned arguments articulated in a lengthy speech but rather on short, interesting sound bites along with carefully crafted images. This is part of the legacy of television, which has changed our habits. When we had only radios, we had to use our imaginations to follow the story line that we were hearing. But when video came along, the images were supplied for us. It is so much less taxing to sit and watch a show than it is to take up a book and read it with any seriousness. This is a real crisis for Christians, because Christians are people of the Word.

Market research once indicated that only 4 percent of Americans walk into a bookstore, either religious or secular, in a given year and actually purchase a book to read. That is, ninety-six people out of a hundred in our culture in a given year never walk into a bookstore and purchase a book for reading. Now, this statistic was compiled before you could buy books on the internet. But that statistic says something about where reading functions in our culture. If you go into your local bookstore and see what the best sellers are—what the 4 percent are reading—that doesn't give us a lot to be encouraged about. The literature that is found in the marketplace reflects the neopaganism of the secular culture.

In Paul's letter to the Philippians, he makes this statement: "Finally, brothers, whatever is true, whatever is honorable, whatever is just, whatever is pure, whatever is lovely, whatever is commendable, if there is any excellence, if there is anything worthy of praise, think about these things" (Phil. 4:8). We are supposed to meditate on things of virtue, which is hard to do when we're reading much contemporary literature. As long as I've been alive, I've been a voracious reader. Long before I was a Christian, I used to read books about sports and the ocean. In fact, when I was a kid, I read every single book in our town's library on sports, even books about Ping-Pong. I didn't care, just as long as it had something to do with sports. The librarian thought I was kind of weird because I just couldn't get enough. If I wasn't out running and playing, I wanted to have a book with me. I wanted to do something.

I still can't sit at a breakfast table without having something to read. If it's only the back of the cereal box, I want to read it.

I have always loved to read. In addition to reading what's in my field, I'm always reading novels, particularly mystery stories. Today, it seems that you can't pick up fiction without being immediately confronted by the most grotesque, vulgar, violent, obscene, prurient literature. In the publishing industry, if they are going to publish fiction, it's as if they have a moral obligation to include within it some kind of salacious material. Many people are addicted to this as a vicarious form of sexual fantasy, to be engaged in reading books of this sort. We have lapsed into a literary form that I call obscene.

Obscene is a very pictorial word, coming from an ancient Greek word meaning "offstage." If somebody was going to be murdered or perish in war in the classical theater, the actors would leave the stage and then somebody would come as a messenger and give the bad news that the character had been slain. Even ancient pagan culture thought it was obscene to show such violence right in front of the audience; it would appeal not to the audience's aesthetic sense but to more base animalistic impulses. The dramatist did not want his art to be compromised by gore and violence. Contrast that with the modern motion picture with its obligatory commitment to gratuitous violence.

There is also pornography. The most shocking displays of sexual content have become routine in our culture. You see it everywhere: in films, on television, in magazines, and in books. The internet has made pornographic videos widely available, of course, but what would have once been considered obscene and unpresentable is now on display in supermarket checkout lines. Prurient content has also filtered down into even the most mundane literature. In one sense, publishing houses are simply giving the public what the market research indicates the public wants and expects, and the public itself is vulgar, and so it expects vulgarity in the written page and in the written expression.

Sometimes people say: "You find earthy language in the Bible. There are vulgarisms in sacred Scripture; even the Apostle Paul, at times, will use a vulgar expression to accent the point he's making." You will never see the Apostle Paul use obscenities or pornography, and the last thing that you would ever find from the pen of the Apostle Paul would be blasphemy.

If there's anything that permeates the modern culture, it is the acceptability of blasphemy in virtually every art form that we encounter in our day. The causal, thoughtless, reflexive use of God's name has become widespread among people in our culture, and especially among artists there is hardly a second thought given to according God's name the respect that it deserves. God is mocked all day long.

Literature is more than fiction, of course. It is also poetry and nonfiction. In these genres, the issue has to do with truth. The postmodern world expects a whole different type of communication, and so we shouldn't be shocked by the way that literature has degenerated, to the point that now there's a great divide between Christian literature and secular literature. In fact, we have two distinct marketplaces: there's the pagan world and there's the Christian world. That has produced a crisis for the American Christian artist. How do you cross that street, how do you penetrate that secular culture, when, in one sense, we've been shut out? That's a question that involves the standards of literature and how they've changed over the years, and what happens when philosophical systems change.

Chapter Seven

Images

As we look briefly at the visual arts in the life of the Christian, we'll first focus on painting. The history of art with respect to painting dovetails with the history of philosophy because artists pick up the reigning philosophical views and articulate them in the way they paint. We have seen that in the ways that postmodernism appears in art in recent decades. Classical art forms are denigrated and destroyed all around us. But my major concern here is not to give a history of art so much as to look at the question of how the visual arts relate to biblical concerns, because I am concerned about how the Christian world has distanced itself from the artists of recent generations. I find it difficult to understand why that is. One possible reason is that Christians view art as worldly and thus as having no place in the house of God.

Beyond that is the church's consideration for the prohibition of certain forms of art found in the Decalogue of the Old Testament. Let's refresh our memories by looking at the second commandment: "You shall not make for yourself a carved image, or any likeness of anything that is in heaven above, or that is in the earth beneath, or that is in the water under the earth. You shall not bow down to them or serve them, for I the LORD your God am a jealous God, visiting the iniquity of the fathers on the children to the third and the fourth generation of those who hate me, but showing steadfast love to thousands of those who love me and keep my commandments" (Ex. 20:4–6).

This is where we find the prohibition against likenesses and graven images. We see how inclusive the prohibition is: we are not to make a carved image of any likeness of anything that is in heaven above or in the earth below or in the waters under the earth. This appears, at least in that context, to preclude the making of any kind of image of anything, either heavenly or earthly. Some Christians have understood the second commandment this way. We know why the second commandment proscribes the production of these images with such severity. One of the most important concerns of God in the Bible is the prohibition against idol worship; idolatry is the most basic and fundamental sin of fallen humanity. In Romans 1, Paul writes of the propensity of all people to exchange the truth of God for a lie and to serve and worship the creature rather than the Creator (v. 25). In this service of worship to the creature, we make all kinds of idols, from the golden calf to totem poles to a host of other representational forms that are then used as deities for worship.

As we saw in chapter 1, John Calvin was concerned to purify worship because he was convinced that worship had declined into superstition and idolatry in the medieval Roman Catholic Church. Calvin wanted to purge all religious imagery, all icons, all statues, all paintings from the life of the church because people were used to bowing down before them, praying to them, and worshiping them.

Calvin was much more concerned about this than Martin Luther was. Luther's chief lieutenant, Andreas Karlstadt, engaged in a radical form of iconoclasm while Luther was at Wartburg Castle. As we saw previously,

Karlstadt destroyed churches and stained glass windows, dragging out the art and ripping it up. When Luther heard about this, he returned to Wittenberg at the risk of his life to stop Karlstadt's overreaction. Luther enjoyed the use of art in the church and in worship. But even Calvin made clear that he did not believe that the second commandment prohibited all forms of art. He stated that the basic concern of the second commandment is the prohibition of idolatry. Calvin said that because the people in the sixteenth century had become so accustomed to praying to idols, it would be wise to get art out of the church. But Calvin believed in principle that having art is permissible.

As we have seen, there is no way to avoid art because every form is an art form, and every art form communicates something. But Calvin made the distinction between rendering images of deity and rendering images of historical and earthly reality, which we call *representational art*. One reason that Calvin allowed for art, at least in principle, is that he couldn't ignore that the same source from which we get the second commandment in the Old Testament is also the source that tells us not only that God allowed artwork to be a part of the people's worship of God and to be part of the tabernacle and temple, but also that He, in a precise, detailed manner, dictated and commanded that artwork be part of the adornment of the tabernacle. For example, the throne of God in Israel that was in the Most Holy Place, the ark of the covenant, was fashioned in gold and had as part of its design two cherubim hovering over or guarding the ark. These angelic beings were fashioned out of gold according to God's direct command.

God also dictated designs for the priests of Israel. In Exodus 28, God tells Moses: "Then bring near to you Aaron your brother, and his sons with him, from among the people of Israel, to serve me as priests—Aaron and Aaron's sons, Nadab and Abihu, Eleazar and Ithamar. And you shall make holy garments for Aaron your brother, for glory and for beauty" (vv. 1–2). We know that God is not only the ultimate source and norm for all goodness and truth but also the ultimate source and norm for *beauty*. Here the living God commands that garments be made for two reasons: for glory and for beauty. Glory, of course, is one of our supreme concerns regarding the nature and character of God. God is to be glorified by His people, and to be glorified means to be treated with dignity and with respect. God's glory refers to the transcendent majesty of God and His august character, which are here linked to beauty. Nobody attaches weightiness or significance to the ugly. This is why it's so important that we understand that the beautiful in art, for example, bears witness to the very character of God, who is the norm of all beauty and the author of all beauty.

This doesn't mean that every painter who paints in a beautiful manner according to the objective categories of beauty that we've looked at—proportion, harmony, complexity, and so on—is intentionally trying to give glory to God. It doesn't even mean that the artist understands the significance of his art.

In Plato's *Meno* dialogue, Socrates interrogates Meno and asks him for the meaning of *virtue*. At the outset, Meno thinks that he understands what virtue is. But under cross-examination, he can't come up with a definition that Socrates can't demolish. Earlier, Plato had written his *Apology*, which contains Socrates' defense against charges that he was corrupting the youth of Athens. While giving his defense, Socrates talked about the quest of wisdom. He talked about seeking out politicians and inquiring of them about the nature of wisdom, and he was disappointed because he couldn't find any wisdom in them. Then he went from the politicians to the artists and craftsmen and then to the poets. When Socrates examined the poets about the meaning of their words or the craftsmen and the artisans about the meaning of their artworks, they could not articulate the ultimate meaning of what they were creating. Socrates was making the point that a person can be really gifted in the political arena, in rhetoric, in poetry, in craftsmanship, or in the visual arts and still have no understanding of ultimate truth.

That is still true today. People can produce things that are beautiful beyond what they themselves understand. I'm not talking here about the subjectivism and existential response to art, in which the artist paints something and you ask, "What does it mean?" and the artist replies: "Whatever you want it to mean. I paint it; you interpret it."

Even the great classical artists such as Michelangelo and Rembrandt would have been stumped by Socrates. They might have been able to testify what they were trying to communicate, but the point is, one doesn't have to be a Christian to bear witness to God. Every work of art that is truly beautiful, whether it's in music, architecture, the visual arts, or literature, bears witness to the character of God, intentionally or unintentionally, because God is beautiful. He's the ground of all beauty. He's the source of all beauty. Even if someone hostile to Him creates an object of beauty, that person is unintentionally giving glory to God.

This is what we see with the garments of the priests. God wants these garments designed for glory and beauty. Note the specific instructions God gave: "You shall speak to all the skillful, whom I have filled with a spirit of skill, that they make Aaron's garments to consecrate him for my priesthood" (Ex. 28:3). Why are these garments there? Not to glorify Aaron, but to set Aaron apart, to sanctify and consecrate him. In a real sense, the beautiful garment covers up the ugliness of the person who is ministering. There is a sense that this points ahead to the fact that we are covered up and adorned by the righteousness of Christ because none of us are worthy to stand on the basis of our own righteousness in the presence of God. We are told that "our righteous deeds are like a polluted garment" (Isa. 64:6). So here God is essentially saying: "When you come into My house, I don't want you coming there in filthy rags. I want you to come dressed in garments that indicate your sanctification, that I have consecrated you, Aaron, and your sons, and that I have set you aside. Why? For the purpose of your office, which is to minister in My presence."

In the last few decades in the church in America, I have seen a radical change in people's clothing style. In Old Testament Israel, before the people came to the holy mountain, they had to spend three days cleaning their garments and making sure they were dressed properly when they entered the presence of God. I know that James tells us that we're not supposed to be snobbish about this and that if a poor person comes into our congregation and can't afford to be dressed up for the occasion, he's not to be ushered out or discriminated against (James 2:1–7). But at the same time, there's this notion that coming into the presence of God is a sacred moment, and so the very clothes we wear in the presence of God are to indicate that state of consecration. We've so changed the focus of church in our day to man rather than God that creature comfort means much more than glorifying God, and so we have a casual attire, which symbolizes something. I ask people to think about the fact that how we dress on various occasions indicates our deepest attitude about the occasion. If we think coming into church is a casual event, then we're going to dress accordingly; if we think it's a holy event, then we're going to dress a little differently.

In Exodus 28, God wants Aaron's garments to look a certain way so that he may minister to the Lord as a priest, and He lists the garments. One of these garments is the ephod: "They shall receive gold, blue and purple and scarlet yarns, and fine twined linen. And they shall make the ephod of gold, of blue and purple and scarlet yarns [these were the most expensive and costly dyes of the ancient world], and of fine twined linen, skillfully worked. It shall have two shoulder pieces attached to its two edges" (Ex. 28:5–7). God gives detailed instructions for how His house is to be built and how His people are to minister before Him. God directs: "You shall make the robe of the ephod all of blue. It shall have an opening for the head in the middle of it, with a woven binding around the opening, like the opening in a garment, so that it may not tear. On its hem you shall make pomegranates" (vv. 31–33). Notice that pomegranates have nothing to do with heaven; they are a representation of earthly things. Is it OK to reproduce flowers in a painting? Of course it is. God uses the common and sanctifies it for uncommon, holy, and sacred usage.

But something even more fascinating is that "on its hem you shall make pomegranates of blue and purple and scarlet yarns, around its hem, with bells of gold between them, a golden bell and a pomegranate, a golden bell and a pomegranate, around the hem of the robe" (vv. 33–34). When did you ever see a blue pomegranate in nature? The artist, by divine instruction, is given permission and authority to transcend the natural by painting blue horses, if you will. Here the seeds of impressionism and expressionism are sown—not by some French revolutionaries but by God Himself, who gives license for artistic creativity in rendering the representative art with these imaginative colors.

Many Christians believe it's OK for art to be used in the church, but they draw the line at images of the divine nature. I don't think that we should try to paint pictures of God in the church, but some in the Puritan tradition and some in the Reformed and Presbyterian traditions go beyond this and say that we should never have any images of Jesus in His incarnation. Many Reformed people will not allow images of Jesus in the art of the church. I'm on the different side of that debate. I fear that such a prohibition wrongly denigrates the humanity of Jesus. When we're painting images of Jesus, we're representing Jesus according to His humanity, just as we might represent the Apostles. We're not trying to capture the divine nature in those representations. There was nothing wrong with Jesus' manifesting Himself with the likeness of human flesh. I don't see anything in Scripture that would prohibit the representation of Jesus according to His humanity in the life of the church. Obviously, any use of art in church runs the risk of degenerating into idolatry, but I believe that the cure for abuse is not disuse. Historically, God has ordained His presence with the beautiful. I think that He has placed a pattern there, a principle that remains forever.

Chapter Eight

Drama and Cinematography

As we continue with our brief overview of the Christian and the arts, we're going to look at the subject of drama and the camera. In the ancient world, drama was an integral part of society. The Greeks had their great dramatists and their presentations of tragedy and comedy. Some of their plays were basically morality plays, and that tradition extended throughout Western history, up to the time of William Shakespeare in England.

But drama as it existed through most of the history of Western civilization took a dramatic turn at the beginning of the twentieth century with the advent of radio, when drama was now broadcast into thousands of homes over the airwaves. Of course, radio dramas lacked the visual dimension. They concentrated chiefly on adventure stories and mystery stories. But radio also became the launching pad for a kind of drama that's become representative of American entertainment: the soap opera.

During the day, soap operas dominated the airwaves. They were called "soap" operas because these little dramas of conflict between people were sponsored by soap companies. These shows represented life situations, precursors to television sitcoms, but they weren't all comedies.

In the evening, radio focused on adventure stories with heroes like Superman, Tennessee Jed, the Lone Ranger, and Captain Midnight. Later in the evening, you had mysteries, such as *Mr. Keen, Tracer of Lost Persons*; *Gang Busters*; *Suspense*; and my favorite, *Inner Sanctum*, which opened with the sound of a mausoleum door creaking open.

The interesting aspect about radio in this era of American entertainment history was that you heard the story but you didn't see it, so the producers of these programs had to create an atmosphere that provoked the listening audience to use its imagination. I can remember as a child listening to these programs and visualizing what was actually going on.

In the middle of the twentieth century came the television, and everything changed. Television has become such a dominant force in our culture that there's a sense that we were caught off guard. No one could really understand or anticipate the revolutionary impact that this medium would have on our culture. The first change seemed at first to be harmless and innocuous. While radio allowed us to project our own imaginations, now the images were produced for us, and we were able to see the images that communicated the story lines or the drama of television. This medium has become so popular and so deeply rooted in the culture that the average child today, by the time he's ten years old, will have seen vastly more drama than any theater lover in ancient Greece or in Shakespeare's England, because this drama is broadcast every hour, every single day.

In the early days of television, much of programming followed the scope of radio programming. We had variety shows. We had children's programs such as *Kukla, Fran and Ollie*, and *Howdy Doody* and all kinds of adventure programs. There were sports, news, and family programs, which were very mild by contemporary standards.

We would see news reports about conflicts around the world in which movie footage was relayed back to the studios and then shown later. Compare that with the experience we have now in which television cameras are posted live in battle scenes and we can watch war happen as it unfolds right before our eyes. Our access to real-time and real-life violence and crime has, in many ways, taken over the medium. Some commentators have observed that we've become a nation that responds not to critical analysis but to sound and video bites.

I think we all know, to some degree, the impact of television on our culture and particularly on the minds of our children, because we know not only that art imitates life but also that life imitates art. The life situations found on television communicate to our children what is basically normative for their experience and their behavior.

Even before the impact of television, we had the movie industry, which also involves drama filmed with a camera. Hollywood's impact on the culture cannot be adequately measured. The film industry was actually pretty tame in the early days. The story lines were quite simple. Basic conflict stories and B-Westerns were the standard fare, and Hollywood was producing hundreds of these movies every year.

When I was a youngster, our local theater showed a double feature on Friday night, a Saturday matinee and a Saturday night double feature, a different double feature on Sunday, Monday, and Tuesday, and still a third double feature on Wednesday and Thursday nights. So if you were an avid theatergoer, as I was, you could see multiple movies in a single week. I went every Saturday and Sunday, so I saw a minimum of four movies a week; sometimes I would go to the Wednesday or Thursday night showing and see six movies in a week. At least four movies every week for about ten years adds up to two thousand movies that I was immersed in as a child.

We would see serialized Westerns with people such as Tom Mix, Tim Holt, and Lash LaRue. The YMCA would show a segment of the serial each week, and we would wait till the following Saturday to see the next episode, and so we had serialized movies. Then they became full-length movies that featured people such as Gene Autry and Roy Rogers. Like actors on television, film characters were idealized heroes who were basically trying to avoid unnecessary violence. The Lone Ranger, for example, was such a good shot that whenever gunplay came into the scene, he would simply shoot the pistol out of the bandit's hand. There was no realistic effort to portray killing or blood and gore and the kind of violence we have in movies today. But that was old Hollywood; an idealized world was set before us in these dramas, in which there was a clear delineation between the good guys and the bad guys. We always knew who the good guy was in the cowboy movies because he wore a white hat and usually rode a white or golden horse. But the bad guys wore the black hats, they had black shirts, and they rode black horses, and so it was easy to know the players even without a program.

But later, with the advent of film noir and the arrival of Method actors such as Marlon Brando, we saw the invention of the antihero. Film became more and more "realistic" as it exposed the seamier elements of human existence, and the idealization of the earlier films was set aside. Several films of this era caused controversy over what they portrayed or sometimes just what they suggested. By today's standards, the objectionable content would seem extremely tame, but at the time it was scandalous.

Many Christians today respond to film simply by withdrawing completely from it, saying that the film industry is so enmeshed in gross immorality, offensive language, and gratuitous sex that Christians should never go to movies. But apart from these obviously offensive things, the film industry has nevertheless been an important artistic medium to communicate important ideas. For example, many people learn the history of earlier eras not through books but through movies. Hollywood has produced important historical war movies, including *A Farewell to Arms* (1932), *All Quiet on the Western Front* (1930), *Sergeant York* (1941), and more recent ones such as *Saving Private Ryan* (1998). Much of what we perceive about what happened in Pearl Harbor and the Civil War comes to us through the graphic portrayals of the film industry. Many of us go through life with those images redounding in our thinking about what life in bygone eras was like. Of course, many of the war movies that were produced during World War II were basically propaganda films to stir up national pride and patriotism in our conflict against the Germans and the Japanese, but they still had value in terms of communicating real-life situations around the world.

Hollywood has also produced important film adaptations of great classic pieces of literature. Who can forget Gregory Peck's portrayal of Captain Ahab in the film version of Melville's epic, *Moby-Dick*? A host of classical literary pieces have been brought to life on the movie screen.

We must realize that films and television programming are shaped by producers and directors. These worlds are created. They're not real; they're imaginary. We understand that films such as *Star Wars* and *The Lion King* (1994) are mythological, but we get caught up in them just the same.

I will never forget watching the first *Rocky* movie. Rocky Balboa, the Italian Stallion, is a down-and-out fighter from Philadelphia who has two chances to win the heavyweight championship from Apollo Creed. Rocky takes the mother of all beatings at the hands of the reigning champion, but he hangs in there. As we watched, we got caught up in the drama of the prizefight. The people in the audience were screaming, cheering Rocky on: "Win, Rocky! Win, Rocky!" We were yelling at the screen, the images coming from a projection machine. There was no Rocky there. It was all make-believe, but we were so caught up in it that we were cheering the hero. I've experienced this when watching a suspense movie, when the bad guy's hiding in the cupboard and nobody knows it except the audience; the heroine doesn't know there's a killer there. We all scream, telling her to watch out—as if she could hear. This is how powerful a movie can be. It involves us emotionally and psychologically by pulling us into another world.

When I was a kid, people had kissing parties. Yes, kissing parties. Boys and girls would come to the party, they'd have refreshments, and then they'd play Post Office and other games. Whenever we had the opportunity to kiss a girl, the moral question that we faced was "Were we going to give the young lady a peck on the cheek, or were we going to kiss her 'Hollywood style'?" This was simply a kiss on the lips that was sustained. That was true romance, and that's the way we learned how to respond romantically. Imagine what today's generation is learning about love, romance, and sex. The thing that's so bad about the sexual activity we see in the movies and on television is the way that it is so casually presented. It's not presented as failure or as conflict or the drama of somebody falling into wickedness, but it's taken for granted that casual sex is part of the American way of life.

We ask: "Does life imitate art? Does art imitate life?" Both are true, and one of the most powerful shapers of worldview in our culture today is the Hollywood movie. That's why I don't think we can afford to ignore it. We need to understand it, and we need to talk to our children about the messages that are being communicated, the worldview that dominates today. Neopaganism is what's being presented to our culture, and it feeds on gratuitous violence, gratuitous sex, and meaninglessness.

Chapter Nine

Architecture

As we near the end of our study of the Christian and the arts, we want to focus our attention on a dimension of art that has historically been important to the church: architecture. From a Christian perspective, we're most interested in architecture as it relates to places of worship. We know, of course, that God can be worshiped anywhere and in any kind of facility. Consider Jacob's experience at Bethel, which means "house of God." While on his journey, Jacob stopped for rest, and while he was sleeping, he had a vision of a ladder that went up to heaven with angels ascending and descending on it. When he awakened, he said: "Surely the LORD is in this place, and I did not know it. . . . This is none other than the house of God, and this is the gate of heaven" (Gen. 28:16–17). Jacob anointed the stone that he had used as his pillow to mark the spot where he had had this encounter with God.

This episode reflects multitudes of similar episodes among the patriarchs and other people of Old Testament redemptive history. They were acutely conscious of the reality not only of sacred time, such as was observed in their festivals, but also of sacred space. We see it, for example, in the Midianite wilderness when God called to Moses out of the burning bush: "Moses, Moses! . . . Take your sandals off your feet, for the place on which you are standing is holy ground" (Ex. 3:4–5). It's sacred space. It was made holy not by the presence of Moses but by the presence of God.

The Old Testament saints were aware of the omnipresence of God. David wrote: "Where shall I go from your Spirit? . . . If I ascend to heaven, you are there! If I make my bed in Sheol, you are there!" (Ps. 139:7–8). The people of the Old Testament understood that no building, no square foot of land could contain the omnipresent God (see 1 Kings 8:27). We are not to think that because the Jewish people had particular places that were set apart, consecrated, and sanctified as sacred spaces, God's presence was limited to those sacred spaces. Rather, because of God's periodic visitation of His people in a redemptive way, these specific places became sacralized, to such a degree that Jerusalem became the Holy City and Israel became the Holy Land, because that is where this intersection took place in redemptive history between God and His people.

In the New Testament, Jesus had a theological discussion with the woman at the well regarding the proper place of worship (John 4). The Samaritans' central sanctuary was on Mount Gerizim, while the Jews had their central sanctuary in Jerusalem. Jesus stated that God is a spirit—that is, He can't be contained to this place or the other place. Those who worship Him must worship in spirit and in truth, and God seeks such people to worship Him in that way (vv. 23–24). Also in the New Testament, we don't find the reproduction of a central sanctuary as in Israel with the tabernacle and later the temple. Christians met for worship wherever they could find a place to do it. The earliest literature indicates that at first the Christians of the first century had small churches that met in people's private dwellings. There is also some evidence that believers gathered secretly in times of persecution in the catacombs beneath Rome. So worship took place outdoors, in people's houses, and even in cemeteries, but there were no established central sanctuaries in the New Testament.

Yet at the same time, the church grew. The church is a corporate body in which people came together weekly for worship and the celebration of the Lord's Supper and so on. Hebrews 10:25 tells us not to forsake assembling together as saints; so whenever a number of people were assembled for worship, prayer, and instruction, they obviously had to have a place where that could occur. The more people who became converts to Christianity, the larger the places needed to be. Church history, very early on, saw the establishment of church buildings to accommodate corporate worship. Church architecture then changed gradually through the ages. No one fixed architectural style stood out from earlier periods to later periods until the Middle Ages, when the Romanesque form of architecture and the beginnings of Gothic architecture in Europe took hold. The Chartres Cathedral became the first real magnificent Gothic cathedral on the Continent. In those days, it could take more than a century to build one of these huge sanctuaries.

In the corporate worship of Old Testament Israel, the most important concept related to the tabernacle or the temple was the *holy*. That's why we have this idea of sacred, holy space. The tabernacle and the temple had the outer court and the Holy Place. Then came the *sanctus sanctorum*, the Holy of Holies, the Most Holy Place, which was the inner sanctum that only the high priest could venture into, and that just once a year. When the medieval church was trying to find a way to express its concept of sanctuary or holy place artistically, it wanted to communicate it in the building itself. Let's briefly consider the pattern that emerged in the Middle Ages for church construction.

Today, cathedrals of this size look to be financially impossible, even though they could be erected in a much shorter time than they were back in the Middle Ages. People in those days wanted to have a cathedral in their town because it became the center not only of religion but of commerce and everything else. If you've been to Europe and seen these cathedrals, you understand why people would be drawn to them.

One of the typical forms for a church building at this time was the cruciform—that is, the church was structured and built in the form of a cross. The entrance place would usually be rather dark. There were side sections to the church, with seating. These sections are called the *transepts* because they represent the horizontal arms of the cross. At the front of the church was the *chancel*, where the preaching was done, the sacraments celebrated, and so on. The main body of the church building, called the *nave*, has an interesting history in the development of church architecture and theology. The church father Cyprian developed the phrase *extra ecclesiam nulla salus*: "Outside the church, there is no salvation." He likened the church of the New Testament to the ark of Noah. For people to survive the deluge during the days of Noah, they absolutely had to actually be inside the ark. They couldn't just be cheering Noah from the shore. They had to be in the ark to survive the flood. Cyprian argued that for a person to be saved today, he has to be inside the visible church. And that center of the church where it all takes place was called the nave, from the Latin *navis*, meaning "ship." The ark of Noah became symbolic for the ship or ark of the church, which was a means of redemption through the waters of regeneration. Churches were built with this meaning and significance in mind.

These cathedrals also featured vaulted ceilings and arched windows. The purpose of a vaulted ceiling was to cause a person's sensory response to be elevated. The idea was that a church building should focus on the character of God, His transcendence, and the sense in which He is high and holy and lifted up. When you are inside one of the great cathedrals of Europe and you look up high, you will see numerous stained glass windows or even rose windows with tiny insets of stained glass depicting moments of redemptive-historical activity. You might see the call of the disciples or the flood or Abraham and Isaac on Mount Moriah. The reason that the beautiful artwork in stained glass is so high and holy and lifted up that nobody can see it is that the beauty contained in these insets is for God, because God can see it. They are for the glory of God. Even down to those details, the architects of these cathedrals were trying to fashion a building that would communicate the nature of God.

If you have ever been in a cathedral like this, you were probably overwhelmed with a sense of awe. The architects thus succeeded at their task, because that's exactly what they set out to do. They set out to construct a building that would artistically communicate the holy presence of God. The Sunday-morning bulletin at our church talks about a transition that takes place when you enter the church. We understand that when people step into the sanctuary, they are symbolically crossing the threshold from the common to the uncommon, from the secular to the sacred, from the profane (which means "out of the temple") into the holy. And that is what church architecture has sought to do for most of the history of the Western and Eastern church.

But after the Reformation, a decisive switch happened in church architecture, when more and more churches were built for more of a utilitarian function to accommodate the needs of the people who assembled. The accent shifted from this lofty, scary, mysterious, transcendent, holy environment to a more comfortable focus on this kind of worldliness, in which the building's primary function is to accommodate fellowship. Churches then started to look more like town halls.

Since then, we've gone through a completely new revolution of church architects, who now design more and more church buildings to resemble a music theater, with the accent on the latest and the greatest in music. The "churchiness" feel of traditional buildings is overcome because people have no sense of the tradition of the church or have rejected the traditional approach to the church. They're not interested in the old, and so the new, innovative building houses a whole different approach to worship.

A church building is an art form, and every art form communicates something. Several years ago, a major bank opened a new branch office in the town where I was living. The first time I walked into the bank, I just looked around. "Wow," I said. The president of the bank was there, and he asked me what was wrong. I said, "Somebody sure put a lot of thought and money into the decor of this building." He wanted to know what I meant. "Well, look around. There are paneled walls, Queen Anne furniture, and Oriental rugs. Everything in this room communicates tradition. The message that you're conveying with your building is that this is a place that's safe; you can bring your money here. We're not going to be taking risks with your money because we are an established, traditional bank." The president replied that I was correct but that I was the first person to notice. I said: "I may be the first person who ever came into this building and said something about it to you, but I guarantee you that every person who steps across the threshold from the street into this bank gets bombarded with the message that you have produced. It's subliminal; people may not recognize it consciously, but it's there, because the architecture that you've chosen does the job."

This is why I ask people in ministry whether they have ever thought about the significance of the design of their church building. I ask whether they've thought about the significance of the design of their office or the design of the Sunday school rooms. Everything we build like this is an art form, and again, every art form communicates something. Your church is therefore communicating a message. You need to find out what that message is, and then you need to ask yourself, "Is that the message we want to convey?" If it is, then the next question is, "Why do we want to convey it?"

I think we have lost the sense of the holy. I don't think that Romanesque or Gothic architecture is the only possible architectural style that can communicate the transcendence, the majesty, and the holiness of God, although I do think it is the best that's been done so far. Again, we know that a building itself, in the final analysis, is not what's going to drive the gospel. It is the gospel that is the power of God unto salvation (Rom. 1:16). But if we want worship to be God-centered rather than man-centered, then we have to think carefully about the design of our sanctuaries.

As we have seen, care is required in our approach to art, especially when it comes to art in the church. There are disagreements on what kind of art belongs in the church, but we cannot remove art from the church completely. That is because every form is an art form, and every art form communicates something. What we should strive for is to imitate God the Creator and to bring Him glory with the art forms we create and the messages that we communicate with those art forms.

About the Author

Dr. R.C. Sproul was founder of Ligonier Ministries, first minister of preaching and teaching at Saint Andrew's Chapel in Sanford, Fla., first president of Reformation Bible College, and executive editor of *Tabletalk* magazine. His radio program, *Renewing Your Mind*, is still broadcast daily on hundreds of radio stations around the world and can also be heard online. He was author of more than one hundred books, including *The Holiness of God*, *Chosen by God*, and *Everyone's a Theologian*. He was recognized throughout the world for his articulate defense of the inerrancy of Scripture and the need for God's people to stand with conviction upon His Word.

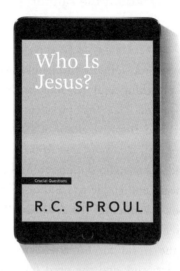

Get 3 free months
of *Tabletalk.*

In 1977, R.C. Sproul started *Tabletalk* magazine.

Today it has become the most widely read subscriber-based monthly

devotional magazine in the world. **Try it free for 3 months.**

Your Questions. Trustworthy Answers.

Have you ever had questions about a passage in the Bible but you didn't know where to go for answers? Has a theological issue sent you searching far and wide for answers you can trust? *Ask Ligonier* is a podcast that allows listeners like you to submit questions about the Bible, theology, the Christian life, and more to trustworthy Bible teachers. Every Thursday, Nathan W. Bingham submits your questions to one of Ligonier Ministries' Teaching Fellows or a special guest. Each teacher draws from years of careful study to provide knowledgeable, accessible answers you can trust.

JUST SEARCH FOR **"LIGONIER MINISTRIES"** IN YOUR FAVORITE PODCAST APP.